HORSE and HOUND

THE HUNTING YEAR

HORSE and HOUND

THE HUNTING YEAR

PHOTOGRAPHY BY TREVOR MEEKS

Commentary by Michael Clayton

HAMLYN

First published in Great Britain in 1994
by Hamlyn an imprint of Reed Consumer Books Limited
Michelin House, 81 Fulham Road, London SW3 6RB
and Auckland, Melbourne, Singapore and Toronto

ISBN 0 600 58506 9

A CIP catalogue record for this book
is available at the British Library

Produced by Mandarin Offset
Printed and bound in Hong Kong

Acknowledgements

With grateful thanks to all Masters, Huntsman, Whips and especially the many hunt followers
and terrier-men without whose help and enthusiasm this book would not have been possible

Trevor Meeks

Foreword

MICHAEL CLAYTON
Editor of Horse and Hound

It was a fortunate day when a young photographer, who had been working for the Press Association on more urban pursuits, expressed a warm interest in taking pictures of equestrian and country sports for Horse and Hound.

Trevor Meeks brought significant technical skills to back his enthusiasm to learn as much as possible about foxhunting. He soon made many friends and exhibited stamina and persistence in tackling the special role of hunting photographer.

Being in the right place at the right time, without interfering with the activities of hound and huntsman at a crucial juncture, requires judgement and experience. Artistry with the camera and stamina are also needed to capture all that is best in our great winter sport.

Soon after Trevor joined us, Horse and Hound posed a new challenge, as it changed its production processes to allow the use of a wealth of additional, up to date colour pictures in every issue.

The hunting field could shine from its pages in all its colourful glory at last. I shall always be grateful to Trevor for his role in assisting our hunting coverage to display the best array of weekly colour action pictures of the Chase available anywhere in the world. The quality of Trevor's photography is clear from the selection of his work presented in this book which is intended to be a cherished addition to the library of foxhunters everywhere. He has accompanied me on a memorable Canadian hunting tour, as well as many in the United Kingdom.

This book celebrates horse and hound in the hunting field - but above all it is a remarkable record of a sport, all too often misunderstood and unfairly abused, which continues to make a valuable contribution to the quality of rural life in the British Isles at the end of the 20th century.

Springtime of Hope

On 1 May the foxhunting year commences; Masters begin their new appointments, and professional Hunt staffs are engaged. Hunt chairmen and committees reflect local support for the Hunt, and are responsible for the financial backing vital to the sport.

It remains the character and talents of Masters and Hunt staff that generate the sport's identity. The cares of a MFH have extended widely since the last 'golden age' of the sport between the wars, when so much of England was still spared the plough and the density of modern roads and traffic. Each spring the foxhunter finishes his season, and assesses the need to rest and perhaps replace horses, saddlery and hunting kit.

Hunt kennels are preoccupied again with the newly arrived whelps, the return of puppies to the pack, and the summering of hunters at grass. In Hunt kennels hounds live in a building known

as a lodge. Each lodge has a bench, raised above draughts, that the hounds sleep on. Bitches and doghounds are kept in separate lodges to avoid indiscriminate

breeding, and there are separate quarters for brood bitches who will be bringing up litters of whelps in the spring and early summer.

When weaned, the young hounds are 'walked' by members of the Hunt. The walkers volunteer to rear the hounds at home, they keep them until the following year when they are returned to the pack.

Hounds are vital, but foxhunting is an equestrian sport for most of those who subscribe to the packs throughout the British Isles. The ability to cross all terrains quickly on horseback is an essential skill for those wishing to be near hounds. Nevertheless, there are packs in hilly and mountainous areas, such as the north-west Fells and the Pennines, that are followed solely on foot.

It is said that some ride to hunt, but the majority hunt to ride. Somewhere between these two extremes lies the truth, as most enjoy watching the hounds and the exhilarating ride in pusuit.

It should be emphasised that the riders are spectators, rather than participants in the hunt. The hunt is the sole responsibility of

the huntsman and his assistants, the whippers-in. It is all too easy for the mounted followers to impede rather than help hounds. Even the scent left by horses can be a nuisance, fouling the ground and masking the scent left by the fox should it run back over land the horses have crossed.

The effective hunter in a good hunting country must be capable of galloping in heavy going, then jumping timber, or hedges and ditches, safely. It must be bold, but temperate in dealing with such modern perils as barbed wire twisted into hedges, or slippery roads laden with traffic, and it should keep its head when performing in company, neither kicking other horses in excitement, nor being deterred from jumping perfectly safe fences because less experienced horses have refused or fallen in front.

Above all, the worthwhile hunter must be sound in wind and limb. It must also be capable of withstanding the stress of regular work in the hunting field throughout a long season, working twice a week, or three times a fortnight at least. No wonder that the foxhunter prizes his mount so highly whether it be top-class thoroughbred, part thoroughbred, cob or pony.

'Letting down' the hunters, transferring them from a diet of hard food and hay indoors to grass out of doors, must be done gradually and carefully. They enjoy the sun on their backs and the freedom to graze after months in stable, but the good hunter always relishes the return to work in the autumn, knowing that a return to the hunting field is nigh.

Spring in the countryside is a time of hard work – Hunt coverts, bridges, gates, fences and rails must all be maintained. Such efforts amount to conservation and benefit both flora and fauna. Foxhunting does not merely take place in the countryside; it is an essential, and firmly entrenched, part of rural life.

Hunt balls, dances, skittle matches, and numerous other social

events will abound during the hunting year. Above all, so many will be looking forward throughout the summer to the summons of the horn and the sweet cry of hounds.

Summer exercise

11

Beagles summering

(Opposite page) The Fernie hounds

A proud mother

Dozing in the sun

First summer

14

Puppy show style

(Right) The day of judgement

16

Spectator sport

Man's best friend

18

Standing in judgement

19

Considered opinion

20

Tea party

21

Hats off for tea

22

Hatstand

(Opposite page) Icing on the cake

Peterborough Royal Foxhound Show

26

Elegance at Peterborough

Signs of success

Professional huntsmen

Dawn of Sport

Sport in the winter owes much to preparation in the summer. The tempo picks up in a foxhound kennel as soon as mounted exercise begins. While the horses are at rest, the kennel bicycle is the huntsman's conveyance when exercising the hounds.

By late July or early August, horses are brought into the Hunt stables for regular work. Some are used to escort hounds on exercise. Such trips are not only to produce fitness; they are educational as the pack includes the young puppies returned to the kennel in the spring, after being 'walked'.

Novice hounds are attached to veterans during exercise, thereby learning discipline and keeping with the rest of the pack during exercise instead of indulging in unofficial expeditions.

Hound puppies are boisterous, intelligent and inquisitive. Those who 'walk' them assist the development of the young hounds physically, by giving them individual feeding and attention, and mentally by affording them the opportunity to make contact with humans while young.

The puppy show, held at the kennels in spring and summer, is an opportunity for the Masters to thank the puppy walkers by inviting them to view the judging of the young hounds. Usually the two judges at a puppy show are an amateur and a professional huntsman.

Doghounds and bitches are shown in two separate classes, since the conformation of each sex is different. Mentally they are different too. Bitches tend to be faster and more dashing, working generously for their huntsman. Doghounds are more dour, extremely persistent, but less forgiving if their huntsman wishes to 'lift' them suddenly onto the line of a fresh fox. A few of the larger packs still hunt separate doghound and bitch packs.

The puppy show is an important event in the rural calendar. On a warm summer afternoon, after a good lunch, with a strawberry and cream tea in the offing, a puppy show is a pleasant social occasion and an opportunity to meet sporting friends, but it is also much more than that.

The puppy show plays an important role in the evolution of the modern foxhound, a breed confined to hounds admitted to the Foxhound Kennel Stud Book, maintained by the sport's ruling body, the Masters of Foxhounds Association, since 1886. Each Hunt keeps records of its own breeding line for inclusion in the stud book.

Hounds are not sold, but are drafted free from one pack to another among the 196 Hunts registered with the MFHA. Bitches are often sent to sires, or stallion hounds, in kennels far afield, helping to provide new bloodlines within each pack.

Hounds are judged primarily on conformation. However, they are working animals, and breeders will want to know that a hound is a top-class performer in the field, whatever its conformation. Breeding specialists take note of the new entry at leading kennels such as the Duke of Beaufort's at Badminton, and the Exmoor kennels of Capt. Ronnie Wallace, who in 1994 celebrated 50 years as a Master of Foxhounds, amateur huntsman and hound breeder.

Hounds from the Beaufort and Exmoor are frequently among those taking leading prizes at the Peterborough Royal Foxhound Show. Their sires, and those of the Heythrop where Capt. Wallace was formerly Joint Master for 25 years, are widely used in foxhound packs throughout Britain, and in North America.

After the work achieved in kennels during the summer, the next stage in the life of the foxhound is the introduction to the hunting field in early autumn. It is in these months that the young hounds learn much in the hunting field. But the language of hunting at this time of year does not always serve the sport well.

Cubhunting, rather than 'cubbing' if you wish to be correct, could to the uninformed conjure images of a small and helpless, furry bundle of foxcub being cruelly pursued. This is not the case.

Foxes born early in the year are fully mature by the autumn, and are virtually indistinguishable from older foxes. The young foxes are living independent, adult lives, and will be engaged on hunting on their own account.

The British Isles has the largest fox population in Europe, but there is no natural predator to cull or disperse them. A pack of foxhounds either kills a fox outright when it is caught above ground, or it escapes unscathed. This is not the case with shooting, trapping, or poisoning, each of which involves the real possibility of a slow, lingering death.

Culling a top predator, such as the fox, is an essential part of its conservation, and hundreds of years of hunting by hounds has produced a thriving fox population in Britain and Ireland.

Apart from the cull, the Hunts perform a vital, conservationist role by planting and maintaining, at considerable expense, the fox's habitat in much of Britain. These fox coverts are areas of copse or small woodland set amid farmland for hunting purposes. They act as habitats for other wildlife, insects and birds, and are beneficial to wildlife in areas where arable farming is widespread.

Young foxhounds learn to hunt by copying older hounds, but the huntsman's success in controlling his hounds is vital too. The hunting horn is not an archaic symbol; it is an important means of communication with hounds. The huntsman finds a fox by 'drawing' a covert, that is by sending hounds into copse, woodland or a stretch of gorse to search for a fox. Hounds hunt by scent, and when a fox is detected, they 'speak' or 'give tongue'.

When cubhunting starts – in late August in moorland countries, or in September elsewhere – hounds meet soon after dawn; they are put into coverts and allowed to hunt at will, perhaps hunting different foxes in groups. They may catch foxes inside the covert, or just outside. The huntsman will encourage them with voice and horn, but will not assemble the pack for a hunt in the open at this stage.

The practice of 'holding up' coverts during cubhunting involves mounted and foot followers standing well back from the perimeter in order to see foxes as they run into the open while hounds are hunting inside the covert. Tapping of whips and shouting is used to discourage these excursions by foxes, but many

persist and escape into open country. Under MFHA rules Masters firmly discourage any attempt at mobbing foxes when they seek to leave covert during cubhunting.

As it is for hounds, the Autumn is a time of education for young horses. Riding your young hunter to the edge of a covert soon after dawn, getting him used to the sight and sound of hounds and other horses is essential to his training.

Sometimes the voices of hounds ring through woodland like an organ in a cathedral. You must keep your young horse clear of hounds and other horses as he may buck or kick in excitement. But if you have the right sort, and have trained him properly away from the hunting field, the young hunter will soon benefit from cubhunting, provided you do not keep him out too long and risk his legs by galloping and jumping on ground which is often hard at this time of year. For this reason, our forefathers saved their top-class horses for the challenge of crossing country on better going from the end of October.

Cubhunting can start in farming areas when the grain crops are harvested, and as the autumn hunting progresses through September and October, meets are held later in the morning.

The huntsman begins to allow hounds out of covert for short hunts in the open. His aim is to have his pack, including the young entry, hunting together. Some of these short, fast hunts in the open during cubhunting are exhilarating. There are fewer followers in the mounted field and one can pick the best grass and hedges in following hounds.

Until the season proper starts, the mounted followers wear 'ratcatcher' dress: tweed coats, fawn breeches, brown or black boots, and bowler hats or caps.

The tempo picks up as the fixtures become later. Autumn rains have usually softened the going by October, and horses may be

galloped and jumped with less risk to their precious tendons. The opening meets are at hand, time for the Chase to don scarlet . . .

32

Hunting at dawn

Watching and waiting

Standing on point

Early risers

36

Ready for the off

Thirsty work

Whipper-in and spectators

(Opposite page) Homeward bound

40

Huntsman's signal

(Opposite page) Drawing for a fox

42

The quarry

Counting in hounds

Spirit of the Chase

The sport achieved in the hunting field is always dictated by the quality of prevailing scenting conditions. The cubhunting meets were held early in the morning during the autumn because hounds find it easier to pick up the fox's scent droplets before the glare of the sun warms up the land.

According to theory, when the ground is warmer than the air, the droplets of scent evaporate less quickly. Later in the season exceptionally good scenting conditions can occur when snow is in the offing and the air is cold. All scenting theories are liable to be exploded by unexpectedly good or bad scent in the most unlikely conditions. It is a major factor in hunting's unceasing appeal to the true enthusiast. No two days are alike and no-one can predict just what quality of sport can be achieved because prevailing scenting conditions hold an element of mystery.

Hunting, whether on foot or on horseback, is always an adventure into the unknown, as so many factors influence the likelihood of hounds finding a fox in the first place, and thereafter achieving a run in the open.

Some hunting folk are inclined to miss meets in areas considered less favourable for a good ride. On these occassions, the faithful can be rewarded by unexpectedly long runs out of the 'bad' country and into the best. These are marvellous hunts in which only a few survive to remain with hounds until the end – with many riders ending up stranded miles from home in the dark.

The autumn, season of 'mists and mellow fruitfulness', is often delightful in the hunting field, but the mists can also arrive as blinding fogs which delay or cancel hunting. Hounds can hunt in a fog, but in the modern countryside a huntsman cannot risk losing touch with the pack if they should suddenly run hard.

Hunters up from grass should ideally be given at least a month's slow road work and a gradual increase in their hard feed diet before entering the hunting field.

The start of the season proper is a time for extra vigilance. Fresh horses kicking and bucking excitedly on their first excursions are all too frequent a source of injuries to mounts and riders.

Rather like a first night in the theatre, an opening meet is anticipated with mixed feelings by the leading members of the cast. 'I'm always relieved when the dratted opening meet is finished with,' said one veteran amateur huntsman at the start of a new season.

'There is too much tension at the opening meet,' he continued, 'and it communicates to the hounds. We get much better sport later in November and December, and certainly we get the longer hunts after Christmas when the ground is colder and the hedges and ditches are bare.'

The official start of the hunting season proper is 1 November, but nowadays many Hunts open their season a little earlier, in the third or fourth week of October, depending on the local harvest.

To fit in with modern farming requirements, the Hunts tend to finish the season slightly earlier than in pre-war years: in mid to late March in farming areas, and sometime in April elsewhere. A few hunts in moorland countries will occasionally hold their final meet during May.

At the opening meet, the mounted field appear in full hunting dress, red coats for male followers entitled to wear the Hunt button, and black for the rest. The ladies wear black or dark blue Hunt coats. Hunting farmers continue to be given the privilege of wearing black coats with black caps. If riders wish, they may wear modern insulated riding headgear with chinstraps, still not popular with some traditionalists but considered by many to be sensible in a countryside littered with hard surfaces on which to fall.

Hunts usually hold their opening meets at a traditional venue where stirrup cups can be dispensed, and where the surrounding country offers the field plenty of fun. The aim now is to hunt the fox in the open, and to follow hounds wherever they may run.

When hounds are put into a covert by the huntsman they will

cast – search with their noses – to find a fox. The huntsman's control with voice and horn should ensure that, when he chooses, the pack unites on the line of one fox, rather than disperses on a number of lines of scent. This is a practice which calls for skill and

experience, but the best huntsmen have an 'invisible thread' of communication with their hounds.

Hounds will hunt in covert, baying or 'giving tongue' when they have found a fox, but the aim is for all the pack to hunt just one fox in the open. While this goes on the mounted field remain in a group well away from the perimeter of the covert.

The whippers-in are strategically placed at corners of the covert. Their task is to view a fox leaving the covert, and once it is clearly running into open country to indicate this to the huntsman with a shout, or 'holloa'. It is then the huntsman's task to ensure the entire pack leaves the covert in one body, hunting the line of that fox. Time wasted at this stage can easily spoil a hunt, because the fox can cover a great deal of country before hounds have even left covert. The fox also seems to know whether scent is good or bad, and will hasten more in good scenting conditions.

True foxhunters have immense respect for the fox. As Jorrocks, the famous fictional Cockney Master of Foxhounds created by Robert Smith Surtees, remarked: 'It ar'nt that I loves the fox less, but that I loves the 'ound more.'

The huntsman sounds the thrilling, doubling notes of 'gone away' on his hunting horn, and if he has educated and handled his pack well during cubhunting they will respond immediately. It is vital that once they hit the scent line of the fox in the open they strike it at an acute angle which impels them to run forward. The mounted field will have heard the holloa and the horn. It is a time to gather the reins for the first hunt of the season. The Field Master will wait until fox, hounds, huntsmen and whippers-in are well away, and will then give the field a lead.

The Chase is on. In some countries, the field will soon be galloping on grass, soaring over timber or hedges. In others they may be tackling steep heather-clad hillsides, or cantering on tracks

alongside vast areas of plough.

The true art of riding to hounds involves staying as near to the pack as possible, but not over-riding them, and certainly not crossing the line they are

hunting. Those who commit such heinous offences may not only be chastised by the Field Master, but might in addition suffer the dire fate of being sent home!

Few hunts in the early stages of the season involve a run without a check. Hounds will temporarily lose the scent of the fox; a good pack casts itself, fanning out to recover the line, but the top-class huntsman will chose the right moment to help them if necessary, casting them with voice and horn towards the direction where his experience and instinct tell him the fox has run. Sometimes he will 'lift' hounds over terrain where scent is bad, such as tarmac or artificially fertilised land, and put them on the line beyond. Many a hunt ends all too soon because the wily fox uses such hindrances to elude hounds.

The hunting day usually consists of a number of hunts, and if foxes are hard to find or scent is poor there may be very long draws between each hunt. A blank day is very rare in modern Britain where the fox population is so large.

In the more expensive Hunts there is often a stop during the day for followers to change to second horses. However in most Hunts nowadays, each rider has one horse and will husband its stamina carefully to remain in the field until he thinks it is time to take it home, whether the huntsman has ended his day or not.

The mounted foxhunter can often see far ahead from a vantage point that is never experienced by car drivers travelling through the countryside. Not only can the rider see over hedges; in a good hunting country he is also able to jump them, thereby attaining a unique freedom of movement.

The skills of riding timber, hedges, drop fences, ditches, and brooks, are born of long experience as well as sheer horsemanship. Most of the best riders start hunting in childhood, and Pony Clubs attached to the Hunts enable new generations of youthful

foxhunters to experience the sport with the benefit of proper guidance.

Hunts encourage the retention of hedgerows, holding hedge laying competitions in many areas, and Hunt

48

staff or voluntary helpers erect timber rails, or triangular contraptions known as 'tiger traps' to enable riders to by-pass the perils of the modern countryside: barbed wire fencing, or back-fencing behind hedges.

The privilege of so much access to farmland is not taken lightly. Hunts appoint at least two subscribers each day as gate shutters, riding at the back of the field to ensure that all necessary gates are shut so that stock do not escape. Fences broken by the Hunt are quickly mended and there is close liaison with farming interests so that growing crops and livestock are unharmed.

As Trevor Meeks' pictures convey, foxhunting is not all of a piece. Our small, crowded island still offers an extraordinary variety of country to be explored on a horse.

The West Country is packed with foxhunting. Cornwall has

grass and banks to be jumped. Devon and Somerset have the moorlands of Dartmoor and Exmoor, and much farmland rich in woodland and copses.

The deep riding Dorset vales offer grass and some of the most daunting hedges and ditches to be found anywhere in Britain. They demand nerve and skill from a horse and rider.

The South and South East contain densely populated rural areas, but foxhunting flourishes, whether in the freedom of the New Forest or the cramped hunting countries of the southern coastal areas further east.

The South Midlands and East Anglia have been hard hit by ever increasing arable farming in the postwar years, which means many acres of plough to be traversed in a hunting day. Yet the Hunts in these areas continue to flourish. Gloucestershire remains a great hunting county, dominated by the Duke of Beaufort's and the adjoining Heythrop pack which produces so much sport amid the grass vales and walls of the Cotswolds.

Motorways, arable farming and modern building development has hit the Midlands, but the great Shires Hunts retain their identities, and all have varying areas which are reminders of the glories of the past when central England was a sea of grass.

Leicestershire is not so fashionable in the 1990s, but it is still a magnet for foxhunters wishing to enjoy cross-country riding at its most delectable. The Quorn's grasslands north and south of Melton Mowbray, the Vale of Belvoir in the Duke of Rutland's country, the grassland south of Oakham in the Cottesmore country, and the Fernie's wonderful grasslands north of Market Harborough, are all areas where foxhunting can be experienced in an East Midlands environment. It was here that Hugo Meynell virtually invented the science of hunting the fox in the open in the late 18th century.

To the west, the Meynell, and the Welsh Borders Hunts such as Sir Watkin Williams-Wynn's, have remarkably unspoilt hunting countries where grass and natural obstacles abound. Foxhunting is a passion for many throughout Wales, and the abundance of grassland, and huge population of foxes, enable the sport to

flourish mightily in hill and valley.

Cheshire and Yorkshire continue their foxhunting traditions despite similar problems to those experienced in the Midlands.

Northumberland and the Borders country retains a wildness and freedom where foxhunting flourishes. In Cumbria's Lakeland they hunt the fox on foot with Fell hounds which tackle the stony slopes in pursuit of the strong Cumberland and Westmorland foxes.

There are only a dozen packs of foxhounds in Scotland but they benefit from less urban pressure than those below the border. Moorland and farmland provide excellent sport, and there are stone walls as well as timber and fly fences to be cleared in such countries as the Duke of Buccleuch's and the Eglinton.

Ireland is a hunting story on its own, with a hugely enjoyable atmosphere, owing much to the uniqueness of the Irish character, the grand stamp of horses to be found in the hunting field, and the special challenges of Irish banks, ditches and walls.

Those who follow the Chase appreciate the diverse beauty of the British and Irish countryside and were conservationist 'greens' long before the preservation of our countryside and wildlife became such an important priority of the late 20th century.

50

Shires opening meet

Ready for action

Taking fly fences

(Opposite page) Whipper-in on duty

54

After a fall

A well earned break

(Opposite page) Hunting in the Borders

Hunt Secretary

Just for fun

Parting company

Huntsman's summons

Working on the line

Hunt jumps

Day's end

All on?

(Following page)
Another day over

The Tynedale

The long trek home

69

(Opposite page)
Cross field and flood

All weather sport

70

Wringing out

After the gallop

Leading the way

(Opposite page)
Special bond

Team work

High Leicestershire

76

Wall country

Time to ponder

After thoughts

(Opposite page) Holloa!

80

Young entry

Pony Club fun

Shetlands south of the Thames

No harm done

84

Irish ditches

Black and Tans

86

Irish banking

Hacking home in Ireland

Master of the Blazers

Resting the hunter

90

Ground frost

White morning

93

Footbound with Foxhounds

95

Border huntsman

(Opposite page) Modern means

East Anglia snow scene

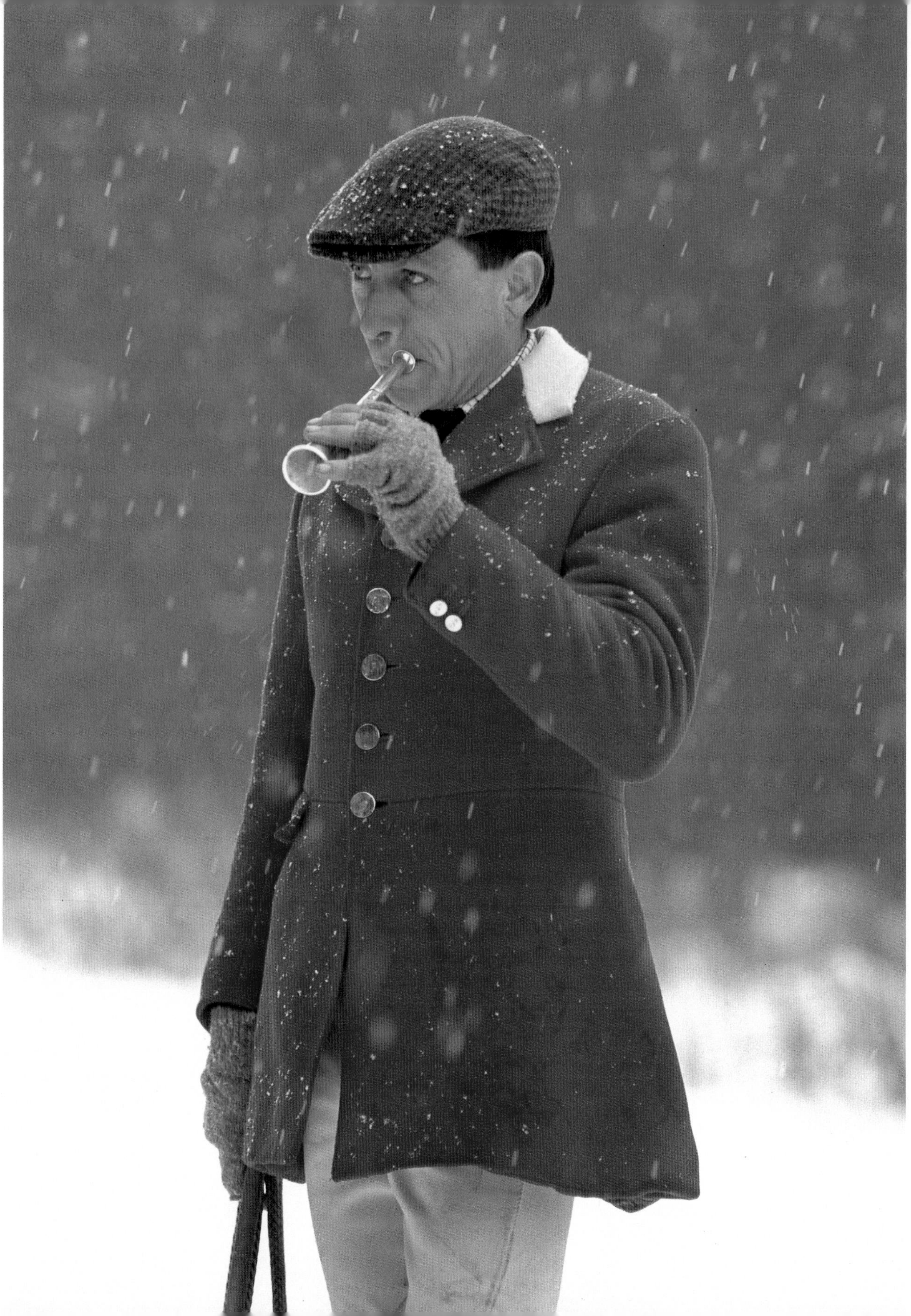

Winter wonderland

(Opposite page) Blowing for home

Horn, whip and crooked stick

(Opposite page) In the Fells

Showjumper in the Chase

(Opposite page) Hound sense

The Ledbury field

Visiting pack

Ready for action

108

Elegance and boldness

Difference of opinion

Good humour

112

'The Gaffer'

113

Gate shutters

Gone away!

115

Special challenge

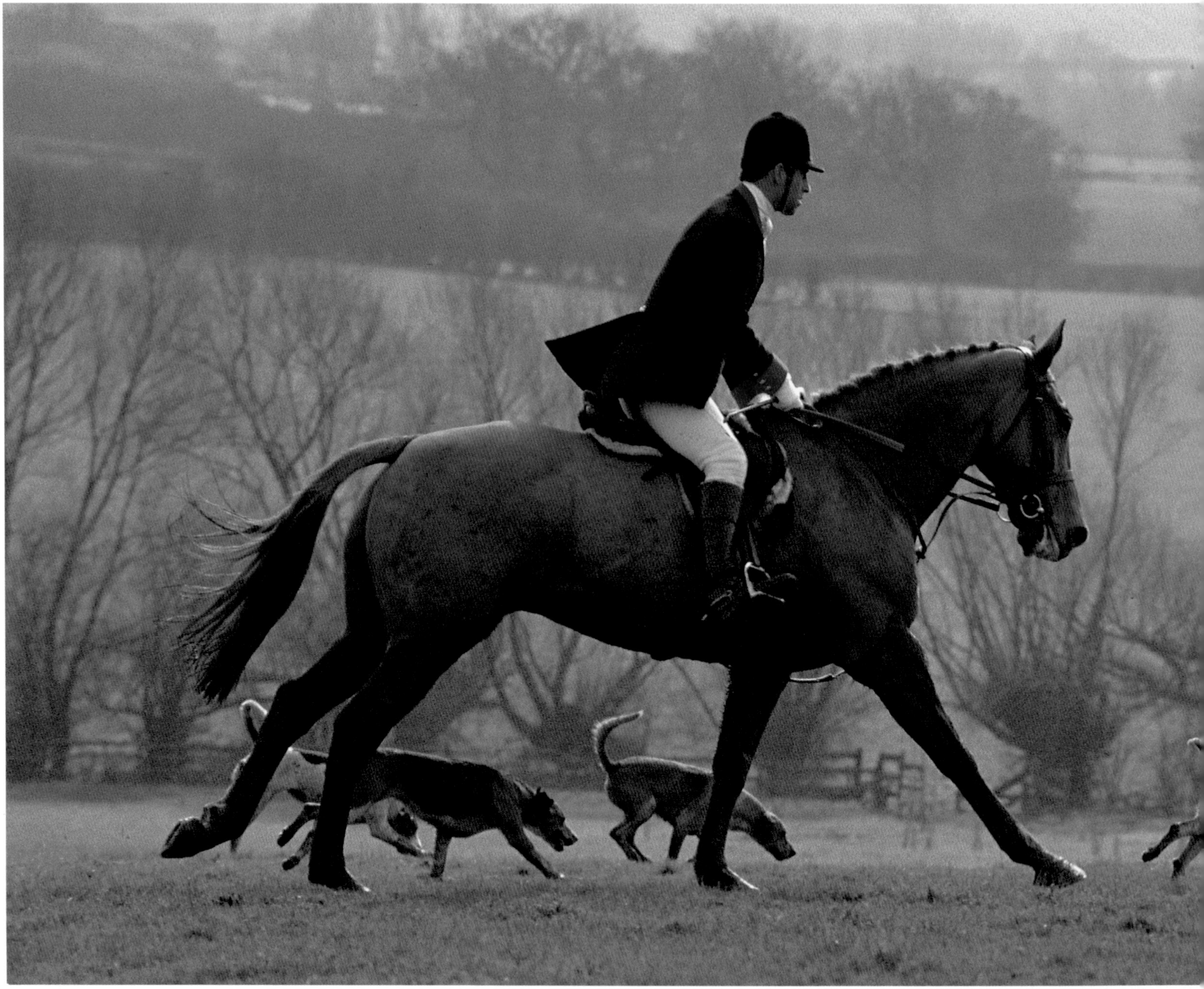

The Prince of Wales

(Following page) Going for it

121

Hounds at sunset

122

Well turned out

(Opposite page) Good Night

Commentary

8-9 Early morning out of season exercise for the Albrighton Hounds, accompanied by their huntsman Paul Barry. The horses are still out at grass, so Paul rides the kennel bicycle. The Albrighton country is in Shropshire and Staffordshire, and hounds meet twice a week.

10 Bruce Durno, veteran huntsman of the Fernie in South Leicestershire since 1962, takes hounds through a water splash during early summer exercise. One of the famous Shires hunting countries, once part of the Quorn, the Fernie is famed for its superb grassland and variety of fences.

11 Mr Nick Herbert, joint master and huntsman of the Newmarket Beagles, exercises hounds through a watersplash during the summer.

12 TOP: Foxhounds are bred to be hard working in the field, and sires and dams are selected only from those registered in the Foxhound Kennel Stud Book. This brood bitch is in the Hampshire 'HH' pack, kept in kennels at Ropsley, near Alresford, Hants.

BOTTOM: Recently born foxhounds are called whelps, not puppies. This couple is part of a litter in the Fitzwilliam Hunt kennel, at Milton, Peterborough. Later in the year they will be sent out to the homes of supporters to be reared. This essential job is known as 'puppy walking'. The following year the young hounds will be returned to the pack, judged and entered for hunting.

13 Whilst in Hunt kennels this whelp's keep is a charge to the Hunt, but soon it will be boarded out with a puppy walker who makes a substantial contribution to Hunt funds by rearing the hound at home.

14 TOP: Hunting runs in families. Mrs Nigel Peel is Joint Master of the North Cotswold Hunt in Gloucestershire and Worcestershire with her husband, who is also an amateur huntsman. Mrs Peel is the daughter of a famous former joint Master of the Old Surrey and Burstow, the late

Mr Uvedale Lambert, and her brother, Stephen Lambert, was a leading Master and amateur huntsman, latterly of the Heythrop.

BOTTOM: Panama hats are popular at the summer puppy shows run by each Hunt. Jeremy Whaley, seen here, was Joint Master and amateur huntsman of the Chiddingfold, Leconfield and Cowdray pack from 1988 to 1994. Their country is in Sussex and Surrey.

14-15 Puppy walkers and other members of the Oakley Hunt observing the young entry being judged at the Hunt's puppy show. Visiting Masters and huntsmen are the judges at these annual shows held during the summer in every Hunt kennel. Those who 'walked' the winning puppies receive prizes.

16 Hound breeding is a science and an art. It is studied with intense interest by the hunting people that make the vital decisions affecting foxhound packs. Mrs Frank Mitchell, in red blazer, was a Joint Master of the Hambledon Hunt, in Hampshire, with her late husband. Hounds are judged on conformation, not colour, and an eye for form is essential at the puppy show.

17 Because they have been reared in the homes of supporters, hound puppies have no fear nor distrust of humans. They are just as biddable as domestic dogs, and extremely obedient. This puppy is taking a break from the judging to come to the ringside to make friends with a spectator.

18 No-one is better equipped to breed and judge hounds than those who have hunted packs for many years. Sharing judging duties at a puppy show are Capt. Charles Barclay, Joint Master and amateur huntsman of the Puckeridge since 1947, and Peter Jones, professional huntsman of the Pytchley since 1971. Capt. Barclay is the third successive generation of his family in the Puckeridge Mastership since 1896. His daughter, Mrs J. C. Pyper, joined the Mastership in 1987.

19   A formidable judging team: Anthony Adams has been huntsman of the Heythrop four-day-a-week pack in Gloucestershire and Oxfordshire, and was trained by the famous former Heythrop Master, Capt. Ronnie Wallace. With Anthony is Capt. Brian Fanshawe, a distinguished Master, huntsman and hound breeder, who finished his career as Joint Master of the Cottesmore in 1992, becoming Director of the BFSS Campaign for Hunting.

20   The convivial, community aspect of foxhunting is seen after a puppy show when everyone is entertained to tea by the Joint Masters. The visiting judges make speeches, and prizes are presented to the puppy walkers who reared the winning hounds.

21   People travel from far and wide to attend puppy shows. They are great opportunities for foxhunters to meet during the summer months. The Hursley Hambledon, where this happy scene was photographed, was formed by the amalgamation of the former Hursley and Hambledon Hunts, as a result of heavy development of roads and buildings in the South Coast area between Salisbury and Petersfield.

22   Bowlers are worn at puppy shows by professional huntsmen who visit as judges or simply attend by invitation. The huntsmen are treated with special respect and have seats allocated to them. After the judging and the tea they usually adjourn to the huntsman's house for further celebration.

23   As in so many rural functions, the ladies of the Hunt rally round to provide sumptuous refreshments. It is all part of the local community's regard for 'our Hunt'.

24-25   Since 1877 Peterborough Royal Foxhound Show has been the world's premier hound show. Hounds from all over the British Isles are entered for this extremely competitive show. The doghound and bitch champions are at the pinnacle of the show, and their lines may be much sought after when breeding decisions are made in kennels. The show takes place at the East of England Agricultural Show's showground near Peterborough in July.

25   TOP: Wearing appropriate headgear for Peterborough Royal Foxhound Show is Mrs Charmian Green, Joint Master of the Warwickshire, who is noted as a hound breeding and judging expert, and was a successful huntsman with the Fox River Valley pack in Illinois, USA.

BOTTOM: Judging hounds in a major show requires considerable experience and a good eye. The shape and movement of the hounds are the basic criteria on which decisions are made. The judges are seeking animals that will withstand many hours of work in the changeable weather of a British winter, and have the quality to move fast in pursuit of an agile quarry. The judges here are Mr Michael Porter, MFH(HH) and Mr Tim Unwin (Cotswold).

26   LEFT: Hunting ladies are encouraged to add elegance to the scene at Peterborough. Mrs Rosemary Stobart is Joint Master of the Tynedale Hunt which has a beautiful grass and stone wall country in Northumberland near Corbridge and Stamfordham. Mrs Stobart was formerly a Joint Master of the Duke of Buccleuch's Hunt on the Scottish Borders.

RIGHT: The rosettes worn on the arm of the huntsman provide colourful signs of success at a hound show. There is much skill in showing hounds in the ring. The huntsman uses his voice, as well as pieces of biscuit, to get his hounds to show themselves at their best. He practises at home to ensure his hounds are not 'shy' in the show ring, a formidable experience for a young hound.

27   Professional huntsmen at Peterborough Royal Foxhound Show: above – Brian Gupwell (formerly, Duke of Beaufort's), Peter Jones (Pytchley), Michael Farrin (Quorn); below – Sidney Bailey (VWH), Tony Collins (formerly Heythrop), Ian Higgs (W. Norfolk), Graham Adams (father of Anthony Adams, Heythrop), and Bruce Durno (Fernie).

32   Before sun up, Vine and Craven followers bring horses in trailers to a cubhunting meet near Newbury, Berkshire.

33   Foot followers are among the keenest foxhunters. Here they wait patiently for hounds to draw a covert at the start of foxhunting at dawn.

34   Patience is important in all field sports, and waiting is as common in foxhunting as galloping and jumping. A follower stands on point, watching for the fox, in the Middleton country in North Yorkshire.

35   Cubhunting is a good time to accustom young horses and ponies to the hunting field. Teaching them to stand patiently at the covert side is a vital part of their education.

36   Martin Thornton, huntsman of the Duke of Rutland's Belvoir hounds, with Joint Master Mr Joey Newton, on the grey, about to start cubhunting in their Leicestershire country.

37   A foxhound can run up to 100 miles during a long day's hunting. Here, a Chiddingfold, Leconfield and Cowdray hound takes refreshment at a cattle trough during a day in the field.

38   One of England's oldest hunting grounds, the New Forest in Hampshire, is still hunted for the fallow buck and the fox. These are the New Forest

126

hounds which hunt the fox, accompanied by their Master and amateur huntsman, Capt. Simon Clarke, after a morning's cubhunting in autumn sunshine.

39 Belvoir first whipper-in Julian Holliday on point duty during a cubhunting morning with this famous Shires pack. Since 1992 Julian has whipped-in for the neighbouring Quorn hounds in Leicestershire.

40 The horn is an essential means of communication between the huntsman and his hounds, and hunt followers. Here it is used during cubhunting by Mr Trevor Adams, Joint Master and amateur huntsman of the Duke of Buccleuch's.

41 Among the most beautiful and varied hunting countries in Britain: the Duke of Buccleuch's occupies huge stretches of moorland and farmland in Roxburghshire, Selkirk and Berwickshire. The Hunt was founded in 1827 and the ninth Duke of Buccleuch has been the senior Joint Master since 1970.

42 The fox, known as 'Charlie' to hunting people, abounds throughout Britain and Ireland. He is a fast, elusive quarry and knows a great deal about the science of hunting himself.

43 Huntsman George Adams 'counting in' his hounds at the Fitzwilliam kennels at Milton, Peterborough, after a morning's cubhunting. Hounds are always counted in couples, and odd numbers are referred to as halves, so that 31 hounds are described as fifteen and a half couple. This practice dates from the days when hounds were coupled together with connecting collars on exercise.

50 The opening meet of the Duke of Rutland's, the Belvoir, traditionally takes place in the village of Long Clawson, lying under the range of hills at the south end of the Vale of Belvoir. The hard riding field enjoy a day of galloping and jumping in the Vale's delectable stretch of pasture and fly fences.

51 Founded in about 1804, the Atherstone is one of the most famous Midlands Hunts, their country falling into the three counties of Leicestershire, Warwickshire, and Staffordshire. Although hit by road developments in recent years it is still a varied country with plenty of sport provided by the Atherstone hounds, seen here ready to start a day's hunting.

52 The Belvoir field going away from its famous covert, Hose Thorns, in the Vale of Belvoir. Mounted fields of well over 100 follow the Belvoir hounds on these popular Saturday fixtures.

53 Ian Jones, whipper-in of the Bicester with Whaddon Chase, on point duty near Ludgershall, Buckinghamshire. The neighbouring Bicester with Warden Hill and Whaddon Chase Hunts amalgamated in 1986 due to urban development, in particular the build up of Milton Keynes.

54 LEFT: Mr Tony Osborne is cheerful after a fall while hunting with the Cotley in the West Country. He wears modern headgear with safety straps.

RIGHT: Samantha Bell, horse trials rider, pauses for quick refreshment before changing horses during a day's hunting in Leicestershire.

55 Mr Bruce Cameron during a long hard day with the Duke of Buccleuch's in the Scottish Borders.

56 LEFT: Mr Peter King, Joint Hon. Secretary of the Meynell and South Staffs Hunt, is well known for exuding calm as well as pipe smoke in his role with this popular Midlands pack.

RIGHT: The Joint Hon. Secretary of the Cambridgeshire, Mrs Julie Findlay, brings cheer to the hunting field.

57 Every country has its challenge. A horse and rider part company in the stone wall country of the Barlow, which hunts the fox in the beautiful uplands of the Derbyshire-Yorkshire borders.

58 Tom Normington, huntsman of the Grafton in Northamptonshire and Buckinghamshire, uses his horn to communicate with hounds. Tom first carried the horn with the Grafton in 1972 and is one of the most experienced and respected professionals.

59 A bitch hound works the line of a fox in woodland in November sunshine. The bitch was part of a private pack, since disbanded, but formerly owned by Mr Kenneth Goschen to hunt in parts of Hampshire and Sussex.

60-61 Bicester with Whaddon Chase followers clearing timber jumps specially erected for jumping. Hunts nowadays invest in carefully constructed timber jumps to avoid the hold-ups that can be caused by barbed wire used in stock control.

62 Members of the Woodland Pytchley mounted field silhouetted against the setting sun at the end of a day in Northamptonshire. The Woodland Pytchley was part of the neighbouring Pytchley until about 1847.

63 Jack Batterbee, huntsman of the West Street Tickham pack in Kent, checks that his pack is 'all on' – still with him – after a hunt. It is the task of the whippers-in to make sure this is the case.

64-65 | The huntsman has 'blown for home' and the Grafton hounds are on their way.

66 | One of the most delightful countries in the north, filled with grass and walls, is hunted by the Tynedale field in Northumberland.

67 | The Radley College Beagles, hare hunters, head for home under a full moon, with their Master and huntsman Andrew Cook, right, and Hon. Secretary James Turner.

68 | George Hyatt hunting the Avon Vale pack across flooded fields.

69 | Mrs John Phillips, wife of the Joint Master of the VWH (the Vale of White Horse) in Wiltshire and Gloucestershire.

70 | Huntsman Ron MacKay wrings out the rain from his coat after a wet December day in Northumberland.

71 | West of Yore mounted field with steaming horses after a gallop during a good day in their country west of the River Yore, in Yorkshire.

72 | Douglas Hunt, huntsman of the Hursley Hambledon since 1978, taking hounds to draw a covert.

73 | West of Yore Joint Master and huntsman Mr Tom Ramsden with hounds. The degree of affection and trust between the pack and its huntsman has a direct bearing on the hounds' performance level.

74 | The Pytchley hounds running together in a hunt. It is essential that a pack works as a team.

75 | Capt. Fred Barker, on the grey, leads the Quorn mounted field alongside The Standard in some of the best of their Monday country. The line of horse boxes in the background indicates the huge number of horses brought out by Quorn followers, most changing to fresh mounts during the day.

76 | The South Notts Hunt has a delightful stone wall country, usually hunted on Thursdays, and lying in the Derbyshire hills.

77 | The Southdown and Eridge was formed in 1981 by the amalgamation of the two neighbouring Hunts bearing these names. Despite the urban development and new roads of the South East, the amalgamated hunt has a varied country affording plenty of sport.

78 | On a short December day when the sun sinks early, an afternoon hunt starts with a fox viewed away – and signalled by the traditional hat in the air, accompanied by the shout of the hunting field, the holloa.

79 | Pytchley huntsman Peter Jones, second right, relaxing with staff at the Hunt lorry after a long day.

80 | Former Joint Master of the Blankney in Lincolnshire, Mr Peter Needham, with his grand-daughter Kate on a leading rein in the hunting field.

81 | LEFT: Thurlow Pony Club member Rosie Bradford.

RIGHT: Zoe Minton, daughter of bloodstock agent Mr David Minton, during a day with the Thurlow in Cambridgeshire.

82 | Shetland ponies among the mounted field with the Southdown and Eridge in South East England.

83 | Pony Club member Chloe Newton, daughter of Mr Joey Newton, Joint Master of the Belvoir, being restored to her pony unhurt after a fall during cubhunting.

84 | Crossing hairy Irish country in pursuit of the Scarteen hounds (Black and Tans) in County Limerick.

85 | The distinctive Kerry Beagles of the Scarteen pack. The pack has been hunted for over 300 years by the Ryan family. It is a daunting country of big banks and wide ditches, but a good Irish hunter will get you across it safely.

86 | Mr Chris Ryan, Joint Master and huntsman of the Scarteen, shows how to negotiate a bank and ditch with balance and style born of long practice.

87 | Hacking home after a day with the Co. Galway (The Blazers) on one of the finest grass and stone wall hunting countries in the world.

88 | Mr Michael Dempsey, Joint Master and huntsman of the Galway Blazers, enjoys an end-of-day whiskey.

89 | Mr Chris Ryan walking with his hunter after a Scarteen day.

90 | A frosty morning in Lincolnshire. In a white frost, scent is often poor but it is still worth looking for a fox on point.

91 | Michael Farrin, veteran huntsman of the Quorn, with hounds during a hard frost in Leicestershire.

92-93 | The East Kent huntsman, Richard Blakeney, is unable to use his horse due to deep snow, but he continues to provide sport, hunting hounds on foot.

94   The Borders pack hunts foxes with much success on hills, and in huge forestry plantations. Hunt staff and followers use horses, and on occasions motorcycles, in order to follow hounds in this extremely challenging country. The Borders pack contains a large element of Fell blood.

95   Mr Michael Hedley, Joint Master and huntsman of the Border Hunt since 1973.

96-97   Thurlow Hunt staff in woodland during heavy snow. Master of the Thurlow, Mr Edmund Vestey, is Chairman of the Master of Foxhounds Association.

98   Former Woodland Pytchley huntsman, Lynsey Hall.

99   Joint Master and huntsman of the College Valley since 1964, Mr Martin Letts, hunting hounds against the snow-clad Cheviot Hills. This Fell-cross pack produces excellent sport in the country now known as the College Valley and North Northumberland, since an amalgamation in 1981.

100   Mr Edmund Porter, Joint Master and huntsman of the Eskdale and Ennerdale with hounds in West Cumbria. These foot packs provide a great deal of sport, and in doing so they perform an extremely valuable fox control service in an area that is heavily dependent upon sheep farming.

101   Equipment for the huntsman with a foot pack. No horse, but a stout stick with a crook to aid progress striding up and down the steep Fells of the North West.

102   Baffle, a Bicester with Whaddon Chase hound, on the look-out during a very wet day while the pack was held up under trees.

103   Towerlands Anglezarke, the great show jumper, after retirement from the ring. He is hunted with the Quorn by Judy Pyrah (second from the right).

104   In the Malvern Hills, the Ledbury's mounted field enjoying a hunt near Bromsberrow. The Ledbury country is in Herefordshire, Worcestershire and Gloucestershire.

105   The Cottesmore hounds have just accounted for a fox during a visit to the Heythrop country by invitation. Capt. Brian Fanshawe, Joint Master and huntsman of the Cottesmore, was retiring from Mastership.

106-107   The Warwickshire hounds await their huntsman's bidding.

108   One of very few ladies hunting side-saddle in the Shires nowadays, Mrs Charlotte Rodriguez, shows how it is done, jumping off a lane over a drop fence in the Quorn Friday country.

109   It was a modest Hunt jump, but the horse said no. There has always been an element of humour in foxhunting. This incident occurred during a day with the North Staffs.

110-111   Cheerfulness and optimism are essential for foxhunting. Both qualities were in abundance among the front rank of the Worcestershire field enjoying a day in February sunshine.

112   Mr Brian Forsyth, seen at the age of 88 following the Warwickshire Hunt on foot. He was formerly an amateur terrier man, and was known as 'The Gaffer'.

113   Binder twine is essential equipment for those subscribers designated as 'gate shutters' during a day's hunting. The twine is used when necessary to make sure gates are firmly shut after the Hunt has passed.

114   Charles Wheeler, kennel huntsman and first whipper-in to the Duke of Beaufort's, holloas away a fox.

115   Taking the big ones as they come. Mr Peter Hill-Walker and Mrs Rosie Butler-Adams following the Bramham Moor hounds. The pack hunts in West and North Yorkshire.

116-117   The Prince of Wales hunting with the Quorn in Leicestershire. Prince Charles started foxhunting in 1975 with the Duke of Beaufort's and enjoyed it immediately. He has since hunted with well over 40 Hunts, large and small, throughout Britain and defends the sport for its contribution to wildlife and conservation.

118-119   Galloping on at a fly fence. The sport of racing over fences was born in the hunting field, and was originally developed in the late 18th century by a Mr Childe from Shropshire who came to Leicestershire to hunt. He developed the practice of flying the fences as they come and was ever afterwards known as 'Flying Childe'.

120-121   The York and Ainsty South hounds in evening light.

122   Traditional hunting wear, still to be seen in the modern hunting field, although top hats are worn less frequently nowadays.

123   Irish hunting field on their way home in the Co. Galway country. Whenever hounds go home it is traditional for followers to wish each other 'Good Night'.